*The Little Book of*

# ANIMALS OF THE ARCTIC

**BUSHEL
& PECK
BOOKS**

ISBN: 9781638191445

First Edition

Printed in the United States

10 9 8 7 6 5 4 3 2 1

# The Little Book of
# ANIMALS OF
# THE ARCTIC

CHRISTIN FARLEY

# Contents

Arctic fox
during winter

## THIS OLD HOUSE

*Arctic foxes can be found to live in dens that have been around for centuries, inhabited from generation to generation. Amazingly, these burrows can include extensive tunnels with up to 150 entrances and can cover hundreds of miles.*

Arctic fox
during
summer

# 1. ARCTIC FOX

Also known as "clowns of the tundra," the Arctic fox is an amusing favorite to find in the Arctic. These solitary animals can also go by "snow fox," "white fox," and "polar fox." Along with an excellent sense of hearing and smell, their ability to move at 30 mph makes them skilled hunters. If birds and rodents are not available, the Arctic fox will dine on carcasses, berries, and seaweed to keep up its nutrition. Their biggest threats are human hunting, wolves, and polar bears. Though their eyesight may be poor, the Arctic fox has adaptations that help protect them, such as a coat that changes colors with the seasons to help them to blend into their environment.

## CLASSIFICATION

KINGDOM: *Animalia*

PHYLUM: *Chordata*

CLASS: *Mammalia*

ORDER: *Carnivora*

FAMILY: *Canidae*

GENUS: *Vulpes*

SPECIES: *V. lagopus*

## BY THE NUMBERS

| | |
|---|---|
| **3-6** YEARS | *Normal lifespan of a fox* |
| **17** POUNDS | *Weight a fox can grow to* |
| **25** | *Largest known number of offspring in a litter* |

### THE PERFECT PELT

*The skin and fur of an Arctic fox, called a "pelt," do an amazing job of keeping the fox warm in the harsh climate. It can resist temperatures of up to -70 degrees Fahrenheit, and as temperatures continue to drop, the fox can increase its metabolism to keep up the heat.*

## PICKY EATERS

*Being as large as they are, you might imagine a walrus feasting on large sea animals. Surprisingly, however, their favorite food is shellfish. Their whiskers help them find shellfish in the dark water, and they can eat up to 4,000 clams in one meal.*

# 2. WALRUS

You might know a walrus by its coarse whiskers, flat flippers, and wrinkled brown and pink skin. If not, the volume of its blubber will surely give away its identity! These traits help them adapt to their frigid surroundings. Their thick skin and blubber act as insulation from the cold, while their flippers aid in helping them move on ice and land. And those unforgettable tusks? They help the walrus to haul their bodies up on ice shelves where they prefer to rest between dives to the seafloor. Resting easily at the top of the food chain, walruses only have two natural predators; the polar bear and the orca are the only matches for the "tusked bull of the sea."

## CLASSIFICATION

**KINGDOM:** *Animalia*

**PHYLUM:** *Chordata*

**CLASS:** *Mammalia*

**ORDER:** *Carnivora*

**CLADE:** *Pinnipedia*

**FAMILY:** *Odobenidae*

**GENUS:** *Odobenus*

**SPECIES:** *O. rosmarus*

## BY THE NUMBERS

| | |
|---|---|
| **40** YEARS | *Lifespan of a walrus* |
| **1.5** TONS | *Maximum weight of a walrus* |
| **3** FEET | *Length a walrus tusk can grow* |

### NEED A NAP?

*While walruses mostly rest on land or ice, they can catch a snooze in the water. They have a "pharyngeal pouch," or air sac, in their throat that fills with up to 50 liters of air and inflates like a pillow. This allows the walrus to doze vertically in the water and keeps them safe from drowning.*

*The hard head of a bowhead whale is not just to house its large, intelligent brain. Their tough noggins also allow them to break through thick slabs of sea ice up to two feet thick.*

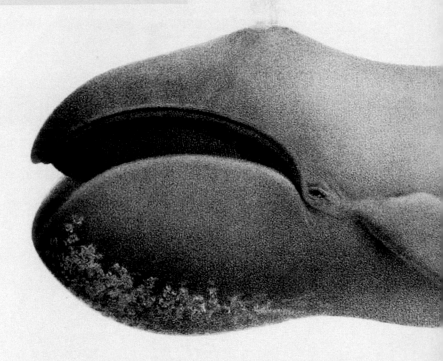

# 3. BOWHEAD WHALE

**B**owhead whales are some of the largest earth animals and are a type of baleen whale. This means they have plates of whalebone in their mouth ("baleen plates") which they use to sift through the water and catch their favorite foods (zooplankton and krill). In fact, they spend the majority of their time underwater with their mouth open in search of food. But don't be fooled—when these large creatures surface, they are still able to leap entirely out of the water! While they tend to travel in small pods of 6-14, they can communicate with each other underwater. Their high-frequency moans, or "whale songs," are used to pass on messages like where to find food.

## CLASSIFICATION

**KINGDOM:** *Animalia*

**PHYLUM:** *Chordata*

**CLASS:** *Mammalia*

**ORDER:** *Artiodactyla*

**INFRAORDER:** *Cetacea*

**FAMILY:** *Balaenidae*

**GENUS:** *Balaena*

**SPECIES:** *B. mysticetus*

## BY THE NUMBERS

| | |
|---|---|
| **200** YEARS | *Years that researchers believe a bowhead whale can live* |
| **100** TONS | *Amount of food a bowhead consumes each year* |
| **60** FEET | *Length a bowhead can become* |

## HOMEBODIES

*Unlike many whale species, bowhead whales do not migrate to warmer waters to feed and breed. They prefer to spend their entire lives in the Arctic waters. They are only found to migrate in the Bering, Beaufort, and Chukchi Seas.*

## DON'T FORGET YOUR VITAMINS

*The indigenous Arctic group, the Inuit, hunt and eat narwhals as part of their diet, and for good reason! One ounce of narwhal skin contains as much vitamin C as an ounce of oranges. Would you add this cuisine to your meals?*

# 4. NARWHAL

Affectionately known as the "unicorn of the sea," narwhals are remarkable creatures if you are lucky enough to see one. The distinguishing feature of the narwhal, its ivory tusk, is actually a tooth! It spirals out of the upper left side of the jaw, protruding through the lip. It's usually the males who develop the tusk. However, scientists have varying ideas of how narwhals use their tusks. These social animals are technically whales and will travel in pods of up to 100. Occasionally, you can find a "super pod" of thousands in shallower water during the summer! Excellent hunters, narwhals feed on deep-sea cod, halibut, and squid. They can stay underwater for 25 minutes in search of their next meal.

## CLASSIFICATION

**KINGDOM:** *Animalia*

**PHYLUM:** *Chordata*

**CLASS:** *Mammalia*

**ORDER:** *Artiodactyla*

**INFRAORDER:** *Cetacea*

**FAMILY:** *Monodontidae*

**GENUS:** *Monodon*

**SPECIES:** *M. monoceros*

## BY THE NUMBERS

| | |
|---|---|
| **10** FEET | *Length a narwhal tusk can reach* |
| **1,500** FEET | *Depth a narwhal can dive* |
| **15%** | *Portion of females that grow a tusk* |

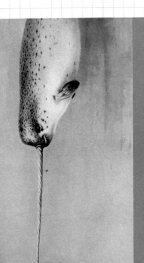

### RARE

*During the Middle Ages, a narwhal tusk was a gift for royalty. It has been said that Queen Elizabeth of England was gifted a carved and bejeweled tusk. Its value was 10,000 pounds, the cost of an entire castle!*

## EXCELLENT EYES

*Arctic hares have amazing eyes and lashes! Due to their eye placement, they can see almost 360 degrees without moving their head. Not only that, but their black eyelashes provide protection from damage caused by sun glare in the winters.*

# 5. ARCTIC HARE

Thick white fur, shortened ears, and a small nose make the Arctic hare an adorable find. But there is much more to the hare than just its charming appearance. Hares are fit to survive the harsh climate by utilizing their long claws to dig up the packed snow. They dig holes under the snow to keep warm and rest, while their keen sense of smell can help them find food buried under the ice. Hares are typically found on hillsides and rocky areas of the tundra where they eat local mosses, woody plants, and lichens. Interestingly, their front incisors never stop growing! While not considered endangered, hares have been hunted by humans for their pelts and have served as meals for foxes and wolves.

## CLASSIFICATION

**KINGDOM:** *Animalia*

**PHYLUM:** *Chordata*

**CLASS:** *Mammalia*

**ORDER:** *Lagomorpha*

**FAMILY:** *Leporidae*

**GENUS:** *Lepus*

**SPECIES:** *L. arcticus*

## BY THE NUMBERS

| | |
|---|---|
| **4** YEARS | *Lifespan in the wild* |
| **37** MILES PER HOUR | *Top speed in miles per hour a hare can run* |
| **6** | *Average litter size* |

### WARDROBE CHANGE

*Twice a year, the Arctic hare will change its body color, and it's not to keep up with fashion. In winter, their white coat helps them blend in with the snow, while their coat turns grayish-brown in the summer. These adaptations help them steer clear of predators.*

**PARTICULAR PALETTE**

*Snowy owls eat birds and small mammals, but their main dietary staple is lemmings! One owl can eat 1,600 lemmings a year! Lemmings have a direct influence on owl productivity. If the lemming population increases, owls will have larger broods!*

# 6. SNOWY OWL

When you imagine an owl, you might picture one perched near the top of a tree. Snowy owls, however, live in the treeless tundra where they can be found on the ground or perched on a post. They are also active hunters during the day instead of at night, making low passes about 3 feet off the ground. The sharp talons on their feet allow them to snatch their prey while in the air. Male and female owls work together to survive and care for their young. The males will hunt while the female stays with the eggs and stores the food the male has delivered to the nest.

## CLASSIFICATION

**KINGDOM:** *Animalia*

**PHYLUM:** *Chordata*

**CLASS:** *Aves*

**ORDER:** *Strigiformes*

**FAMILY:** *Strigidae*

**GENUS:** *Bubo*

**SPECIES:** *B. scandiacus*

## BY THE NUMBERS

| | |
|---|---|
| **4** FEET | *Average wingspan* |
| **10** YEARS | *Lifespan in the wild* |
| **6** POUNDS | *Maximum weight* |

### BYSTANDER BEWARE

*While they look friendly, it's best to keep your distance from a snowy owl. They are fierce defenders of their territory and have been known to dive-bomb humans and attack Arctic wolves. Breeding season is their most aggressive time, so observe these majestic creatures with binoculars!*

## POWER IN NUMBERS

*Musk oxen move in herds as an added protection against predators, their main enemy being wolves. One defense tactic is to "circle the wagons," which is when the oxen circle around their young with their horns faced outward. Unfortunately, it has not been effective against human predation, and now they are a protected species.*

# 7. MUSK OX

It's been said that a musk ox looks like a dust mop with feet. This humorous description highlights the thick, two-foot-long hair of the ox that keeps it warm during the fierce cold. One of their most important traits is this double coat of fur. The shaggy outer hair covers a shorter wool undercoat called a "qiviut." Although they look similar to buffalo, the musk ox is more closely related to sheep. Their main food sources come from grasses, lichen, roots, and any available shrubbery. Even today, they are occasionally domesticated for their milk, meat, and wool.

## CLASSIFICATION

**KINGDOM:** *Animalia*

**PHYLUM:** *Chordata*

**CLASS:** *Mammalia*

**ORDER:** *Artiodactyla*

**FAMILY:** *Bovidae*

**SUBFAMILY:** *Caprinae*

**TRIBE:** *Ovibovini*

**GENUS:** *Ovibos*

**SPECIES:** *O. moschatus*

## BY THE NUMBERS

| | |
|---|---|
| **18** | *Number of oxen in a herd* |
| **37** MILES PER HOUR | *Top speed of a musk ox* |
| **20** POUNDS | *Weight of a musk ox at birth* |

### HEAVY WEIGHTS

*We know from their appearance that musk oxen boast an intimidating stance. But how big is big? A male can reach 900 pounds, which is as much as an adult horse. A female can get up to 500 pounds in weight, comparable to the weight of a grand piano.*

## BUZZ OFF

*Apart from the threat of large predators, caribou are also susceptible to attacks from biting insects called warble flies. The larvae can penetrate the caribou's skin, causing a parasitic infection in the milk, meat, and hide. Thankfully the FDA approved a drug to treat these infections called "ivermectin."*

# 8. CARIBOU

Caribou are large mammals in the deer family and, depending on where you live, are also known as "reindeer." They are the fifth largest species in the family, and both males and females will shed their antlers each year. Unlike other deer species, they have fur that completely covers their noses that is beneficial in the Arctic to warm the incoming air. Social animals, caribou will live together in small herds and migrate thousands of miles each year in their search for food. Once spring rolls around, they can form super-herds numbering into the hundreds of thousands! When they are on the move, they can reach speeds of 50 mph, so keep out of their way!

## CLASSIFICATION

KINGDOM: *Animalia*

PHYLUM: *Chordata*

CLASS: *Mammalia*

ORDER: *Artiodactyla*

FAMILY: *Cervidae*

SUBFAMILY: *Capreolinae*

TRIBE: *Odocoileini*

GENUS: *Rangifer*

SPECIES: *R. tarandus*

## BY THE NUMBERS

| | |
|---|---|
| **18** POUNDS | *Amount of vegetation an adult can eat in a day* |
| **1** | *Average littler size* |
| **5+** MILLION | *Number of caribou in the world* |

## AMAZING ANKLES

*One surprising fact about caribou is the superpower of their ankles! Each ankle has a special gland that releases an odor when there is a nearby threat from predators. The smell sends a message to the other caribou to leave and protect themselves.*

## OLYMPIC STATUS

*While it's more common to see polar bears wandering slowly and waiting patiently for a seal to grab, they are actually very fast! They can run faster than the quickest Olympic sprinter! You don't see them in stride very often, however, because they are prone to overheating.*

# 9. POLAR BEAR

**P**olar bears are fascinating for a myriad of reasons. Not only are they the world's largest bear species, but they are also the only species classified as a marine mammal! This is because they spend the majority of their lives on the sea ice. In fact, they can swim at speeds of six mph for hours to get from one ice shelf to another. To keep up their body weight, they have to consume over 12,000 calories a day by feasting on seals or scavenging for carcasses of smaller mammals. Patient hunters, they will wait until a seal comes up for air to attack.

## CLASSIFICATION

**KINGDOM:** *Animalia*

**PHYLUM:** *Chordata*

**CLASS:** *Mammalia*

**ORDER:** *Carnivora*

**FAMILY:** *Ursidae*

**GENUS:** *Ursus*

**SPECIES:** *U. maritimus*

## BY THE NUMBERS

| | |
|---|---|
| **26,000** | Total worldwide polar bear population |
| **1,500** POUNDS | Mature weight of a male polar bear |
| **41** YEARS | Age of the oldest polar bear on record |

### FASCINATING FUR

*Your jaw might drop open when you learn that polar bears are not actually white! Their fur is translucent and appears white when it reflects the light. Underneath all that bushy fur, their skin is actually dark black!*

# 10. ARCTIC GROUND SQUIRREL

The Arctic ground squirrel is the largest type of ground squirrel and is only found in North America. They make their home in forests, grasslands, and tundra of Alaska and Northern Canada. Here, they can feed on grasses, flowers, seeds, insects, and even animal carcasses, all while trying to keep clear of foxes, grizzly bears, and falcons. Males are larger than females, though each has the same powerful limbs and cylindrical shape. Summer is a glutenous time during which the squirrels must increase their body fat by 40% in preparation for hibernation. Males work diligently to store nuts and grasses in their chambers for when they awake, and females begin their winter sleep early.

## CLASSIFICATION

**KINGDOM:** *Animalia*

**PHYLUM:** *Chordata*

**CLASS:** *Mammalia*

**ORDER:** *Rodentia*

**FAMILY:** *Sciuridae*

**GENUS:** *Urocitellus*

**SPECIES:** *U. parryii*

## BY THE NUMBERS

| | |
|---|---|
| **10** WEEKS | *Time it takes for new squirrel pups to be independent* |
| **30** DAYS | *Time of gestation for new pups* |
| **5** | *Average number of pups in a litter* |

## LITERALLY FREEZING

*Arctic ground squirrels hibernate for seven to eight months out of the year. During this time, their brain and body temperatures drop below freezing! Through a method called "supercooling," squirrels can keep their blood from freezing, allowing them to stay alive. After hibernation, it takes three hours to regain consciousness, and by the next day, they are back to normal!*

# 11. RIBBON SEAL

The distinctive pattern on the skin of a ribbon seal easily sets it apart from other seals. Four light-colored, ribbon-shaped markings contrast against their dark-gray or black skin. You are most likely to find them in Arctic regions of the North Pacific Ocean, where they prefer a solitary life in deep ice waters. Here, they can live for 25-30 years if undisturbed, enjoying a life filled with fish, crustaceans, and other marine creatures. Diving for food is also a must; meals like squid, shrimp, and octopus help fulfill their demanding diet of up to 20 pounds of food a day.

## CLASSIFICATION

KINGDOM: *Animalia*

PHYLUM: *Chordata*

CLASS: *Mammalia*

ORDER: *Carnivora*

CLADE: *Pinnipedia*

FAMILY: *Phocidae*

GENUS: *Histriophoca*

SPECIES: *H. fasciata*

## BY THE NUMBERS

| | |
|---|---|
| **210** POUNDS | *Weight they can reach* |
| **1** | *Number of pups a female will birth each year* |
| **650** FEET | *Depth they can dive* |

## MODERN MOVEMENT

*If you didn't recognize the ribbon seal from its unique coloration, you will know it by its movement on the ice. While most seals move in similar motion to a caterpillar, the ribbon seals show off their own style. They will move their hips and head in a side-to-side motion and alternate flipper strokes to propel themselves forward.*

## MAINSTAY MEAL

*Unfortunately for the bearded seals, they are a staple on the dinner menu for walruses, polar bears, and killer whales. They are a high-calorie meal and help keep up the body mass of such predators. Thankfully, the bearded seal can reproduce in numbers to keep themselves off the endangered species list.*

## 12. BEARDED SEAL

**B**earded seals are one of the four seal species found in the Arctic and the largest of any seal on Earth. They are characterized by their square-shaped flippers and unusually long whiskers. Bearded seals are not social animals and tend to keep to themselves outside of mating season. While they try to avoid interaction, males do sing underwater songs to attract a mate. Their diet consists of fish, octopus, crabs, and clams. Long whiskers aid their search for food in more shallow waters. And if they need to rest, they can sleep vertically in the water with their head just above the surface.

### CLASSIFICATION

**KINGDOM:** *Animalia*

**PHYLUM:** *Chordata*

**CLASS:** *Mammalia*

**ORDER:** *Carnivora*

**CLADE:** *Pinnipedia*

**FAMILY:** *Phocidae*

**GENUS:** *Erignathus*

**SPECIES:** *E. barbatus*

### BY THE NUMBERS

| | |
|---|---|
| **500,000** | *Number of bearded seals in the world* |
| **30** | *Lifespan of a bearded seal* |
| **8 DAYS** | *Length of a mature bearded seal* |

### THEY GROW UP SO FAST

*Life is harsh in the wild, and bearded seal pups have to grow up fast. Born on ice floes, they weigh about 70 pounds and enter the waters hours after birth. Mothers care for them for about three weeks, during which time the pups consume eight liters of milk daily and quickly become excellent divers.*

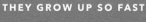
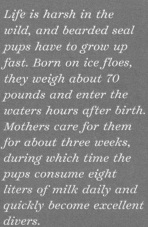

## BOOGER BLISS

*Researchers are on the hunt for beluga boogers. Yes, you heard that right, they want beluga snot! Interestingly, their snot contains hormones that give scientists clues to their wellbeing. The hormones provide information on the stress levels of beluga whales and may help determine the causes of their stress.*

# 13. BELUGA WHALE

**B**eluga whales are the most vocal of all whales, earning them the name "canaries of the sea." They can make various vocal sounds, from high-pitched whistles to chirps and bleats that communicate information to one another. The word "beluga" means "white" in Russian, which is a bit ironic; beluga whales are born gray, and eight years go by before they turn completely white. Like other Arctic whales, belugas do not have dorsal fins, but they do have the characteristic thick blubber layer. Though they are technically a "toothed whale," they swallow their meals of squid, crabs, snails, and shrimp whole. They might not be fast swimmers, but they make up for it with their majestic backward swim.

## CLASSIFICATION

**KINGDOM:** *Animalia*

**PHYLUM:** *Chordata*

**CLASS:** *Mammalia*

**ORDER:** *Artiodactyla*

**INFRAORDER:** *Cetacea*

**FAMILY:** *Monodontidae*

**GENUS:** *Delphinapterus*

**SPECIES:** *D. leucas*

## BY THE NUMBERS

| | |
|---|---|
| **800** METERS | *Depth a beluga can dive* |
| **60** POUNDS | *Amount of food a beluga can consume each day* |
| **3** YEARS | *Number of years between pregnancies* |

### LIFE SAVER

*Mila, a Beluga whale in captivity in China, saved a 26-year-old free diver who plunged into the Arctic pool during a competition. The frigid temperature of the water paralyzed the diver's legs. Sensing the distress, Mila came to her rescue, pushing the helpless diver to the surface.*

## LIGHT ON THEIR FEET

*The Canada lynx has an ingenious adaptation to its arctic lifestyle. Unlike wild cats like cougars, the lynx has natural snowshoes for feet. With round feet and a wide-angled big toe, they can distribute their weight to allow them to better stay on top of snow. This key trait also allows them to hunt at higher altitudes in deeper snow.*

# 14. CANADA LYNX

Native to North America, the Canada lynx is also known as the North American lynx. Twice the size of a house cat, their fur colors range from gray to reddish-brown. Their long legs give them the appearance of being quick on their feet. However, Canada lynx are not fast hunters, preferring to wait for their unsuspecting prey and pounce!

## CLASSIFICATION

**KINGDOM:** *Animalia*

**PHYLUM:** *Chordata*

**CLASS:** *Mammalia*

**ORDER:** *Carnivora*

**SUBORDER:** *Feliformia*

**FAMILY:** *Felidae*

**SUBFAMILY:** *Felinae*

**GENUS:** *Lynx*

**SPECIES:** *L. canadensis*

## BY THE NUMBERS

| | |
|---|---|
| **12** YEARS | *Lifespan of a Canada lynx in the wild* |
| **37** POUNDS | *Weight of a mature lynx* |
| **3.5** FEET | *Length of a mature lynx* |

## COMMON CUISINE

*Imagine eating the same meal everyday—that might get old quick. The Canada lynx doesn't seem to mind that the snowshoe hare makes up 90% of its diet. Occasionally, it will consume birds, small mammals, or deer, but it always returns to its favorite!*

## SERIOUS STORAGE

*Thanks to their spiny palates and coarse tongues, puffins can keep a firm grip on 10-12 small fish in their bills at one time. This allows them to bring back food for their young in one fishing trip. In comparison, other seabirds must swallow and regurgitate their catch for their young.*

# 15. PUFFIN

Standing at just ten inches tall with striking colors and a pudgy body, it's no wonder that puffins are one of the most adorable sea birds! They've earned the nickname "clowns of the sea" for their awkwardness on land and their clown-like faces. One trait that sets them apart is their technicolored beaks. The coloring only lasts for the spring breeding season and will change to a dull-colored beak as winter comes around. Puffins are a hard-working breed despite their poor flying abilities. They have to beat their wings 300-400 times a minute to stay in flight, which usually ends in a crash landing. Luckily, they are excellent swimmers and divers, allowing them to secure their fish dinners.

## CLASSIFICATION

**KINGDOM:** *Animalia*

**PHYLUM:** *Chordata*

**CLASS:** *Aves*

**ORDER:** *Charadriiformes*

**FAMILY:** *Alcidae*

**TRIBE:** *Fraterculini*

**GENUS:** *Fratercula*

## BY THE NUMBERS

| | |
|---|---|
| **60%** | Percentage of the world's puffin population that breeds in Iceland |
| **500** GRAMS | Weight of a mature puffin (about the same as a can of soda) |
| **1** | Number of eggs a puffin lays each year |

### FAMILY TIES

*Family relationships are important to puffins. They usually pair up and mate for life, with some relationships lasting for 20 years! In spring, they take turns incubating their single egg. Over the course of the summer, they work together to raise their chick and later return to the same burrow with their mate.*

**SAFETY ZONE**

*The Arctic wolf is the only subspecies of wolf that is not threatened. Being in such an isolated part of the globe helps secure their well-being as a species. In the Arctic, few mammals can survive. The Arctic wolf's only predator is the polar bear or the occasional threat from another wolf for mating or territory rights.*

# 16. ARCTIC WOLF

Arctic wolves are well-adapted to the world's harshest climates. This subspecies of gray wolf can tolerate temperatures as low as -30 degrees Fahrenheit in places like Alaska, the Arctic Circle, and Iceland. Compared to other wolves, the Arctic wolf has a shorter muzzle, smaller ears, shorter legs, and year-long white fur. Traversing the frozen ground is no problem thanks to furry paws that help insulate from the cold and provide more traction. Keen senses of sight, hearing, and smell make the wolves proficient hunters. They will travel in packs for up to ten hours a day, hunting their preferred musk oxen and Arctic hare.

## CLASSIFICATION

**KINGDOM:** *Animalia*

**PHYLUM:** *Chordata*

**CLASS:** *Mammalia*

**ORDER:** *Carnivora*

**FAMILY:** *Canidae*

**GENUS:** *Canis*

**SPECIES:** *C. lupus*

**SUBSPECIES:** *C. l. arctos*

## BY THE NUMBERS

| | |
|---|---|
| **40** MILES | *Distance an arctic wolf covers each day while hunting* |
| **20** POUNDS | *Amount of meat an arctic wolf consumes each day* |
| **150** POUNDS | *Average weight of a mature arctic wolf* |

## SOCIAL STATUS

*Arctic wolves have a complex hierarchy when it comes to their social interactions. The pack has a dominant male and female who both stand tall and carry their tails high to let everyone know who is in charge. Body language, scent marking, and various vocalizations help to maintain the hierarchy.*

**MATERNITY MATTERS**

*Moose young are called "calves," and their mothers are often referred to as "cows." Their pregnancy is a lengthy 243 days, after which one to two calves are born (with the occasional third). The calves can weigh as much as 33 pounds and quickly gain about three pounds a day.*

# 17. MOOSE

If you've ever wanted to see a moose, your best bet is to visit Canada. Here resides the largest population of the total two million moose worldwide. These normally docile creatures are the largest of the deer species and tend to live solitary lives (except during mating season). Naturally, moose don't have many enemies, though gray wolves and bears are known to target the old, young, and sick. Unfortunately, moose are prone to infection, and a bite from a predator can be what does them in. Fortunately, their massive, 50-60-pound antlers and sharp hooves can help fend off attacks. Moose can live up to 25 years in normal conditions, but due to human hunting, the average has decreased for males to 10-20 years.

## CLASSIFICATION

**KINGDOM:** *Animalia*

**PHYLUM:** *Chordata*

**CLASS:** *Mammalia*

**ORDER:** *Artiodactyla*

**FAMILY:** *Cervidae*

**SUBFAMILY:** *Capreolinae*

**TRIBE:** *Alceini*

**GENUS:** *Alces*

**SPECIES:** *A. alces*

## BY THE NUMBERS

| | |
|---|---|
| **7.6** FEET | *Height of a mature moose* |
| **1,800** POUNDS | *Weight of a mature moose* |
| **70** POUNDS | *Amount of food a moose consumes each day during the summer* |

### SUPER ATHLETES?

*Due to their size, you might think that moose are slow-moving. Myth debunked! They can run up to 35 mph, keeping a steady trot at 20 mph. Plus, they are incredible swimmers! Moose are able to swim several miles at a time and hold their breath underwater for about 30 seconds.*

## BALANCING ACT

*Dall sheep are astonishing! Living on cliff edges, they can balance on an edge only two inches wide! Not only that, but they can climb a mountain at 15 mph and bounce up to 20 feet in the air. Now that would be a sight to see!*

# 18. DALL SHEEP

Steep mountain cliffs and on dry knolls are where you are most likely to locate a Dall sheep. You'll recognize them from their thick gray-white or black fur coats and large, curly horns. Females ("ewes") have smaller horns compared to their male counterparts ("rams"). The two groups have a unique relationship. Females and their young live separately from males in populations called "groups" until breeding season. During this season, the males will slam and kick each other with their horns to prove their dominance. Luckily, the Dall sheep have air "cushions" in their head to prevent brain injuries with all those kicks to the head.

## CLASSIFICATION

**KINGDOM:** *Animalia*

**PHYLUM:** *Chordata*

**CLASS:** *Mammalia*

**ORDER:** *Artiodactyla*

**FAMILY:** *Bovidae*

**SUBFAMILY:** *Caprinae*

**TRIBE:** *Caprini*

**GENUS:** *Ovis*

**SPECIES:** *O. dalli*

## BY THE NUMBERS

| | |
|---|---|
| **154** POUNDS | *Weight of a mature Dall sheep* |
| **12-16** YEARS | *Average lifespan of a Dall sheep in the wild* |
| **1** | *Number of lambs born to a sheep each year* |

## HUNGRY FOR THE HUNT

*Alaskan residents and non-residents enjoy hunting Dall sheep. Their meat is a common part of the local diet, and they are used as trophy animals. Due to their limited natural predators, the Dall sheep population is steady, and they are legal to hunt in regions of Alaska to keep their population in check.*

## POPULOUS POSTERITY

*Greenland sharks don't start reproducing until about age 150! The gestation period lasts from 8-18 years. That is a long pregnancy for a female shark. Due to their extensive lifespans, Greenland sharks can have 200-700 pups in their lifetime!*

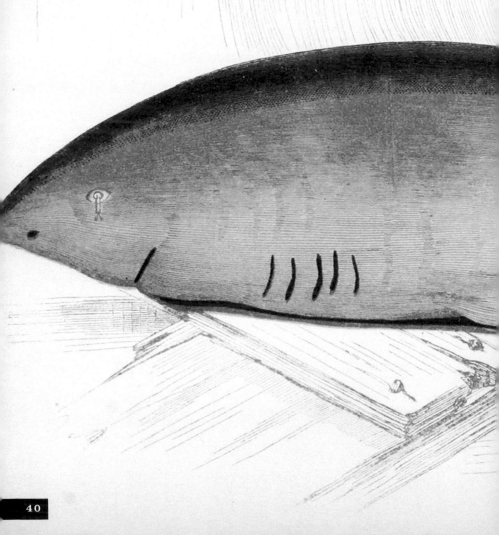

# 19. GREENLAND SHARK

Greenland sharks make the record book for being the longest-living known vertebrates, living up to 400 years in the wild, according to scientists! Unlike their namesake, these sharks are not only found in Greenland but are found from North America to the East Siberian Sea. They are known as "sleeper sharks" and move slowly through the water with stealth. Human encounters are rare, but they eat like nature's garbage disposal. They are content with pretty much any flesh—dead or alive. With about 50 upper and lower teeth, Greenland sharks have little difficulty grasping and crushing their prey. Inhabiting frigid water temperatures and, at times, extreme water depths, your chances are thankfully low that you'll ever come face to face with this shark.

## CLASSIFICATION

**KINGDOM:** *Animalia*

**PHYLUM:** *Chordata*

**CLASS:** *Chondrichthyes*

**SUPERORDER:** *Selachimorpha*

**ORDER:** *Squaliformes*

**FAMILY:** *Somniosidae*

**GENUS:** *Somniosus*

**SPECIES:** *S. microcephalus*

## BY THE NUMBERS

| | |
|---|---|
| **3,100 POUNDS** | *Weight of a mature Greenland shark* |
| **24 FEET** | *Length of a mature Greenland shark* |
| **10** | *Average litter size* |

### DINNER DANGER

*Shark meat is widely consumed by humans. However, think twice about eating a Greenland shark. Their meat is toxic to humans, causing severe intestinal problems and inebriation. But have no fear—when properly fermented or dried, the meat becomes edible and is even considered a delicacy in Iceland.*

### FREQUENT FLYERS

*Tundra swans pack on a lot of flight miles each year when traveling from their winter to summer homes. Summers are spent in the Canadian Arctic and Alaska before they then fly over 3,700 miles to their winter destination. This can be to the mid-Atlantic Coast or as far as the Central Valley of California. Making this arduous flight twice a year is an impressive feat!*

# 20. TUNDRA SWAN

Tundra swans are characterized by their snowy white plumage, black feet, and black bills with distinctive yellow markings. These long-necked beauties can be found in flocks and spread-out during breeding season. Breeding takes place in the Arctic, where young swans will mate for life and build a nest near a lake or pond. It is constructed of sticks lined with grasses and moss. When migration time comes, the swans will form their iconic V-shaped formation, racing at speeds of up to 100 mph. The sound made from the powerful beating of their wings in flight led to their other title, "whistling swans."

## BY THE NUMBERS

| | |
|---|---|
| **5.5** FEET | *Average wingspan of a mature tundra swan* |
| **20** YEARS | *Average lifespan of a tundra swan in the wild* |
| **4** | *Number of eggs laid by a swan each season* |

### DEFENSIVE PARENTING

*The Arctic is home to fierce predators who are always on the hunt for food. Swan parents are usually successful at warding off predators such as foxes, weasels, and other birds. For larger predators like bears and wolves, the parents don't stand a chance. They will quickly flee the nest in order to draw attention away from the nesting area.*

## ALL ABOUT THE LEFTOVERS

*The scientific name for a wolverine is* Gulo gulo, *meaning "glutton." This is fitting, as a wolverine has a voracious appetite and a one-track mind when it comes to food. They have been known to steal food from animals like bears or bury a leftover carcass in the snow to preserve it for later. Meat is not the only thing on the menu—a wolverine will devour the bones too!*

## 21. WOLVERINE

Sometimes, the wolverine gets a bad rap with nicknames like "skunk bear" or "nasty cat." Sure, their anal scent glands are potent and pungent, but there is so much more to them than meets the eye (or nose)! About the size of a medium dog, wolverines have their own superpowers. They are immune to poisons from scorpions and snakes, have incredibly strong claws, and have a remarkable sense of smell. With a dense fur coat that can repel water and frost, they are fit for the numbing Arctic cold. In addition, they have greater endurance than marathon runners. They can cover a territory range the size of half of Rhode Island!

### CLASSIFICATION

**KINGDOM:** *Animalia*

**PHYLUM:** *Chordata*

**CLASS:** *Mammalia*

**ORDER:** *Carnivora*

**FAMILY:** *Mustelidae*

**GENUS:** *Gulo*

**SPECIES:** *G. gulo*

### BY THE NUMBERS

| | |
|---|---|
| **42** INCHES | *Length of a mature wolverine* |
| **20** FEET | *How deep a wolverine can smell food in the snow* |
| **16** YEARS | *Average lifespan of a wolverine in the wild* |

### TO THE RESCUE

*Wolverines are now being used in search-and-rescue operations thanks to their ability to smell far under the surface of snow. They can be trained to sniff out humans who have been victims of an avalanche. Researchers say they are smarter and easier to train than dogs.*

### CRAFTY WITH THEIR CATCH

*It's no wonder orcas have the second heaviest brain of marine mammals. They are keen hunters that can trick their prey. They've been known to purposefully slide onto the shore to scare sea lions into the water where other orcas patiently wait. Deliberately causing waves to throw their prey off ice floes into the water is an orca tactic that they even teach their young!*

# 22. ORCA

Enchanting imagery of an orca as a playful and gentle marine animal might make you smile. However, what most don't know is that orcas are ferocious predators who, with their impressive intelligence, live at the top of the food chain. Their dinner menu consists of pretty much anything—from sea lions, sharks, and squid to other whales and even penguins. Interestingly, besides humans, orcas are the only species to have a form of culture. Scientists have found that each family, or "pod," has its own learned behavior and even dialect that they can pass on from generation to generation. These elegant and intriguing creatures are sure to amaze the human family for generations as well.

## BY THE NUMBERS

| | |
|---|---|
| **60+** YEARS | *Lifespan of an orca in the wild* |
| **500** POUNDS | *Amount of food an orca can eat each day* |
| **34** MILES PER HOUR | *Swimming speed of an orca* |

## WHAT'S IN A NAME

*Orcas also go by the name of "killer whales," though they are technically members of the dolphin family. The nickname was originally switched to "whale killers" because nearby sailors saw them hunting whales and other marine life.*

# 23. ARCTIC WOOLY BEAR CATERPILLAR/ MOTH

A s the oldest caterpillar on Earth, the Arctic wooly bear caterpillar is as hardy as it is ancient. About one to two inches in length, the wooly bear is covered in soft brown and black hair. What is remarkable about this insect is that it spends seven years freezing and thawing in the Arctic environment and still manages to survive! In fact, 90% of their lives are spent in frozen hibernation thanks to an antifreeze agent in their bodies that protects their tissues from temperatures as low as 70 below zero. The other 10% of their lives is spent trying to consume as much food as possible during the short warm season.

## PARTY TIME

*Yearly festivals, the largest of which is held in Vermilion, Ohio, celebrate the wooly bear. Why have a party for a caterpillar you might ask? Beginning in 1973, people have commemorated the mythical connection between the wooly bear and winter. There are even competitions between caterpillars to size up their speed and endurance.*

## CLASSIFICATION

**KINGDOM:** *Animalia*

**PHYLUM:** *Arthropoda*

**CLASS:** *Insecta*

**ORDER:** *Lepidoptera*

**SUPERFAMILY:** *Noctuoidea*

**FAMILY:** *Erebidae*

**GENUS:** *Gynaephora*

**SPECIES:** *G. groenlandica*

## BY THE NUMBERS

| | |
|---|---|
| **7** YEARS | *The time it takes for the caterpillar to develop into a moth* |
| **75%** | *The percent of wooly bears that die from parasitic wasps and flies* |
| **14** | *The lifespan a wooly bear can reach* |

# 24. ARCTIC WOLF SPIDER

The Arctic wolf spider is similar to other wolf spiders but is endemic to Greenland. Webs are not their specialty since they hunt on the ground, but their eyes are a BIG deal—literally. Two eyes are large and noticeable, while four smaller ones sit just below. The remaining two eyes are spaced out on top of their head. Unlike human eyes, wolf spiders cannot move their eyes side to side but must move their bodies to view what they want to see. This doesn't deter their hunting abilities. Like wolves, these spiders are excellent hunters even at night and enjoy a diet of insects like springtails.

## CLASSIFICATION

**KINGDOM:** *Animalia*

**PHYLUM:** *Arthropoda*

**SUBPHYLUM:** *Chelicerata*

**CLASS:** *Arachnida*

**ORDER:** *Araneae*

**INFRAORDER:** *Araneomorphae*

**FAMILY:** *Lycosidae*

**GENUS:** *Pardosa*

**SPECIES:** *P. glacialis*

## BY THE NUMBERS

| | |
|---|---|
| **1.6** INCHES | *Average length* |
| **2** YEARS | *Average lifespan* |
| **1** OUNCE | *Average weight of an adult* |

## NINJA SPIDERS

*With stealth and speed, wolf spiders will pounce on their unsuspecting prey. These athletic creatures then grab their prey and roll over on their backs while holding it with their legs. After injecting the prey with venom that liquifies its organs, the spiders will drink their meal. And to think this is all done in the dark of night!*

## CURIOUS COURTSHIP

*Mating rituals commence with a "high flight" during which the female follows the male to high altitudes. This is followed by a slow descent together to the ground. If that encounter goes well, the male will offer the female a fish and strut his feathers with lowered wings and raised tail. Finally, they are officially a couple when they fly around and circle each other.*

# 25. ARCTIC TERN

The Arctic tern is characterized by its gray and white plumage, a red bill, and a black "cap" on its head. Medium in size with short, red legs, terns are known worldwide for their migration. They are record holders for having the longest known migration in the animal kingdom. Travel takes them from the north in Greenland down south to the Weddell Sea off the shores of Antarctica. In fact, some Arctic terns will travel about 1.5 million miles in their lifetimes. Thankfully, they spend a lot of time in the air gliding instead of constantly flapping their wings. For refreshment, terns can sleep while gliding or dive bomb to catch fish in rivers or oceans.

## CLASSIFICATION

**KINGDOM:** *Animalia*

**PHYLUM:** *Chordata*

**CLASS:** *Aves*

**ORDER:** *Charadriiformes*

**FAMILY:** *Laridae*

**GENUS:** *Sterna*

**SPECIES:** *S. paradisaea*

## BY THE NUMBERS

| | |
|---|---|
| **2** | *Average number of eggs laid by a tern in a breeding season* |
| **34** YEARS | *Age of oldest surviving terns* |
| **25** MILES PER HOUR | *Flight speed of a tern* |

## WATCH YOUR HEAD

*Terns become fiercely defensive if their nest and young are threatened. If humans or other large predators venture too close, terns will strike the top or back of their heads. The attack won't cause serious damage, but it may draw blood, discouraging outsider visits.*

*One of the benefits to living on the edges of cliffs is that there are few natural predators— they are the only gull to make cliff dwellings. With remote nest locations, kittiwake chicks do not require camouflage like other species and are born white. Natural instincts also teach chicks how to stay still so as to not fall off their cliff.*

, F.Z.S.

# 26. KITTIWAKE

**K**ittiwakes are the most numerous breed of gull in the world. Their name comes from the sound of their calls—"kittee-wa-aaake!" Social birds, kittiwakes will nest together on cliff ledges in colonies that number into the thousands. Here, they find lifelong mates and work hard to build their nests of seaweed, feathers, mud, and barnacles. Food is plentiful right by the nesting grounds. They are known to eat a diet of small fish that they can grab from the surface of (or just below) the water. Their most common prey includes cod, herring, and sand lance. Special glands desalinate their blood, allowing kittiwakes to drink salt water.

## BY THE NUMBERS

| | |
|---|---|
| **4** | *The years it takes for them to mature for breeding* |
| **5** | *Weeks old a chick will be before it can fly* |
| **18 MILLION** | *Estimated world population* |

### FINICKY FEEDERS

*Kittiwakes are expert fishermen; maybe that is why they can afford to be picky about the food they feed their chicks. Adults will store food in their "crop" (pouch) that they will regurgitate to feed their young. However, any food that lands on the nest while feeding will not be eaten but instead be plucked up and dropped down the cliff's side.*

### HELPFUL BIRDS

*Long ago, St. Kilda residents found many uses for fulmar birds in Scotland. Fulmar eggs, skin, feathers, and meat contributed to the way of life for the native people. The bones of the fulmar were also used as jacket fasteners. Whatever was left of the birds was then used to aid in fertilizing their fields.*

## 27. FULMAR

It is easy to get a fulmar confused with a gull due to their gray wings and white bodies, but they are actually related to the albatross. Superb gliders, fulmars will brave storms and rough ocean weather that other breeds avoid on their coastline refuge. Similar to kittiwakes, fulmars live in colonies on Arctic island cliffs. They mate for life and return to their same nests every year during the breeding season. When it comes time to feed, fulmars are capable of diving for food, but they prefer to catch their prey on the surface or scavenge for leftovers. Main fulmar staples include jellyfish, squid, fish, and other animal carcasses.

### CLASSIFICATION

**KINGDOM:** *Animalia*

**PHYLUM:** *Chordata*

**CLASS:** *Aves*

**ORDER:** *Procellariiformes*

**FAMILY:** *Procellariidae*

**GENUS:** *Fulmarus*

### BY THE NUMBERS

| | |
|---|---|
| **6-12** | *Age in years they breed at for the first time* |
| **17** | *Length in inches of a fulmar* |
| **2** | *The weight in pounds a fulmar can reach* |

### SMELLY SECRETION

*Survival is difficult for any young animal, and a fulmar chick is no exception. To defend themselves while the parents search for food, a chick can fend off predators like gulls and falcons. They spit a foul-smelling oil—a stomach secretion—as a defense mechanism. The substance can matt the feathers of attackers and affect their thermoregulation.*

*Another name for an Arctic skua is "parasitic jaeger." The parasitic part comes from their habit of stealing food from other animals called "kleptoparasitism." On the other hand, "jaeger" is a German word meaning "hunter," describing its natural predator instincts.*

# 28. ARCTIC SKUA

Arctic skuas are medium-sized birds similar to gulls. They come in two color variations—a gray back with a white underbelly or a uniformly dusky brown. Both types have two pointed central tail feathers that extend beyond their main tails and flashes of white under their wings. What makes the Arctic skua memorable is its tendency for piracy. Most of their diet comes from stealing the food of other animals. Puffins and terns, for example, will be chased by skuas in hopes that they will drop their fish for an easy meal. As a result, skuas survive just fine on their own and prefer to live a solitary life away from other birds.

## CLASSIFICATION

**KINGDOM:** *Animalia*

**PHYLUM:** *Chordata*

**CLASS:** *Aves*

**ORDER:** *Charadriiformes*

**FAMILY:** *Stercorariidae*

**GENUS:** *Stercorarius*

**SPECIES:** *S. parasiticus*

## BY THE NUMBERS

| | |
|---|---|
| **12** | *Average lifespan in years* |
| **30** | *Length in days of incubation period* |
| **50** | *Flight speed in miles per hour* |

### HOME BASE

*The lakes and coasts of the Arctic tundra are home to skuas during the summer months. Here, they stay to breed and help incubate the eggs with their mate until the young are born and able to provide for themselves. Once winter rolls around, it's off to warmer climates as far as South America or South Africa.*

## HERBIVORE HUNT

*During winter months, pink-footed geese tend to gather near farmlands and can wreak havoc on local crops. Some governments have stepped in to both aid the geese and ensure the safety of the farmers' fields. Measures have included leaving harvested beet tops and other leftover crops out for an easy target for geese, hoping to keep them away from growing plants.*

# 29. PINK-FOOTED GOOSE

If you live in Svalbard, Norway, a pink-footed goose is a common sight. They are the most common goose in this area of the world. They have a gray-brown body, well-known pink feet, and a pink middle marking on their short, black beaks. Like a kittiwake, the pink-footed goose breeds on rocky outcrops and cliffs but can also be found in open Arctic tundra anytime it feels safe from hungry predators. Nests are generally shallow divots in the ground lined with feathers and plants. The female will lay three to six eggs with the sole responsibility of tending to them. Males remain nearby to guard the breeding area.

CLASSIFICATION

KINGDOM: *Animalia*

PHYLUM: *Chordata*

CLASS: *Aves*

ORDER: *Anseriformes*

FAMILY: *Anatidae*

GENUS: *Anser*

SPECIES: *A. brachyrhynchus*

## BY THE NUMBERS

| | |
|---|---|
| **27** | *Average length in inches* |
| **20** | *Average lifespan in years* |
| **500,000** | *Approximate global population* |

### WIDE RANGES

*Pink-footed geese can gather in groups of thousands. These social flocks have several names: a blizzard, a knot, a plump, a string, and a chevron. While flying at speeds of 35 mph during migration, they can also cover 130,000 square miles!*

### FRIENDLY COMPETITION

*When both of your neighbors have a similar diet, it can cause some competition in the bird world. Razorbills, guillemots, and puffins all share the same menu but have worked out their differences. Puffins catch small fish, razorbills catch medium-sized fish, and the guillemots go for the larger catch. Problem solved!*

# 30. RAZORBILL

Unlike other Arctic bird species, razorbills are found exclusively in the North Atlantic. They differ from other bird species with their jet-black back feathers and white undersides, along with the white line that extends from their eyes to their bill. Such a bill is sharp and shaped like a hatchet to aid in catching fish underwater. Their diet is mostly made up of fish, crustaceans, and marine worms. A male razorbill will usually stay near his chicks while they learn to hunt for food on their own. Although they may look similar to penguins, razorbills are actually the closest living relative of the great auk (now extinct).

## CLASSIFICATION

**KINGDOM:** *Animalia*

**PHYLUM:** *Chordata*

**CLASS:** *Aves*

**ORDER:** *Charadriiformes*

**FAMILY:** *Alcidae*

**GENUS:** *Alca*

**SPECIES:** *A. torda*

## BY THE NUMBERS

| | |
|---|---|
| **41** | Oldest known razorbill in years |
| **330** | Depth in feet they can dive in the ocean |
| **15** | Average length in inches |

### NO FEAR

*When razorbills hatch, they usually find their home on a cliff hundreds of feet above the sea. Twenty days after birth, they are ready to leave the nest, but their wings are not yet fully developed. Amazingly, they will jump from the nest with no hesitation, fluttering their wings to slow their fall to reach the sea!*

## HOT IS HARMFUL

*Muskrats prefer wet areas and cool burrows to call home. In fact, areas with four to six inches of water are ideal! Dry and hot climates are detrimental to muskrats. Luckily, they are equipped with a special mechanism called "regional hyperthermia" that helps regulate the blood flow to their tail and cools their body core.*

# 31. MUSKRAT

Though they may be mistaken for beavers, muskrats are a smaller semi-aquatic rodent, weighing only between two and five pounds. They are related to other rodents like rats, hamsters, and lemmings with their rounded bodies, short legs, and even smaller ears. Though muskrats can live worldwide, those that live in the Arctic region are native to North America. As omnivores, muskrats enjoy a plant-based diet of local vegetation. In the event that food becomes scarce, they will feed on insects, fish, and amphibians. If times become even more dire, muskrats have been known to resort to cannibalism!

## BY THE NUMBERS

| | |
|---|---|
| **8** | *The number kits born to a muskrat each year* |
| **8** | *The number of litters they can have a year* |
| **1/3** | *The portion of their body weight in food they must consume a day* |

## OVERCROWDING

*Sometimes, it's just time to leave the family home. With multiple litters a year and a number of new additional kits, the family home can get cramped. After six weeks, a kit is fully grown and able to take care of itself. Though they may prefer to stay with the family, it's not uncommon for the mother to kick the grown kit out!*

### CLEAN-UP CREW

*Even though they will plunge underwater to catch a fish, ivory gulls are opportunistic feeders. In other words, they don't mind letting the larger animals do more of the work. For instance, the gulls will follow polar bears, hoping to clean up any leftovers from their kill. Ivory gulls are anything but picky. Fecal matter and placentas of other mammals are delightful finds!*

# 32. IVORY GULL

The scientific name for the ivory gull, *Pagophila eburnea*, is telling. "Pagolphila" means "lover of sea ice" and "eburnea" means "ivory-colored." You can identify these birds from their brilliant plumage, blue-green bills with yellow tips, and black legs. Since they live the furthest north of any bird species, these gulls inhabit areas of open water surrounded by ice, called "polynyas." When mating season rolls around, they are flexible on nesting sites. The ivory gulls will nest with their monogamous mates on floating ice blocks, cliffs, and high mountains. Parents work together to raise their chicks but tend to live solitary lives after the breeding season.

## CLASSIFICATION

**KINGDOM:** *Animalia*

**PHYLUM:** *Chordata*

**CLASS:** *Aves*

**ORDER:** *Charadriiformes*

**FAMILY:** *Laridae*

**GENUS:** *Pagophila*

**SPECIES:** *P. eburnea*

## BY THE NUMBERS

| | |
|---|---|
| **2** | *years before their full plumage comes in* |
| **1.5** | *average weight of a gull in pounds* |
| **60** | *highest number of breeding couples a colony will house* |

## AFRAID OF THE DARK?

*Unlike many Arctic birds, the ivory gull does not truly migrate. Instead, they stay put throughout the dark winter months in the harsh climate. If they do transition, they will only move as far south as they need to in order to avoid complete darkness.*

### "WHITECOATS"

*Pup harp seals are born with pure white fur, earning them the nickname "white coats" at birth. This fluffy white coat helps the pups stay warm and absorb sunlight since their blubber is still developing. A valuable adaptation for the pup, their fur coat is also highly valued in the fur trade; therefore, they need to be protected.*

## 33. HARP SEAL

Greenland hosts the greatest population of harp seals, though they also live off the coast of Russia and Newfoundland, Canada. These earless seals get their common name from the harp-shaped marking on their backs. Life for the harp seal is mostly spent in the Arctic water, but they come on the ice surface to court, birth, and rear their young. With a migratory route of over 3,100 miles round trip, the seals consume a diverse diet of at least 67 fish species and even more invertebrates. Shallow waters are preferable, but harp seals are known to dive to a depth of 400 meters for food. While on the hunt, they have to be mindful of the walruses, sharks, whales, and polar bears that are looking for a seal meal.

### CLASSIFICATION

**KINGDOM:** *Animalia*

**PHYLUM:** *Chordata*

**CLASS:** *Mammalia*

**ORDER:** *Carnivora*

**CLADE:** *Pinnipedia*

**FAMILY:** *Phocidae*

**GENUS:** *Pagophilus*

**SPECIES:** *P. groenlandicus*

### BY THE NUMBERS

| | |
|---|---|
| **16** | *Minutes a harp seal can stay underwater at a time* |
| **7.5** | *Estimated harp seal population worldwide* |
| **1** | *The number of pups born at a time* |

### PUTTING ON THE POUNDS

*Getting enough food is essential for young pups to survive in the wild. They need plenty of blubber and fat storage to insulate their bodies. Luckily, seal mothers provide a high-fat milk diet that allows the pups to gain over four pounds a day! This allows them to reach the healthy weight of 250-300 pounds in no time!*

## WINTER LIFE

*Life in the frigid cold can cause some species to hibernate in order to survive. Lemmings are one of the local Arctic species that does not hibernate. Instead, they spend their winters under the snow in burrows and tunnels lined with grass, hair, and moss for comfort. In fact, the snow above their burrows acts as an insulator for greater warmth.*

# 34. LEMMINGS

A lemming is not your everyday rodent. It may look like a small guinea pig or a mouse, but it is not afraid to show its true colors. In fact, its fur can be a mix of colors, making it more conspicuous to predators. And if a predator approaches, a lemming is not afraid to fight back! Three lemming species make their home in the Arctic, enjoying the treeless tundra and subarctic grasslands. They live solitary lives with the exception of when they are breeding, spending at least six hours a day making up for the low-calorie diet that plants provide. Lemmings spend the rest of their time under the snow in burrows.

## CLASSIFICATION

**KINGDOM:** *Animalia*

**PHYLUM:** *Chordata*

**CLASS:** *Mammalia*

**ORDER:** *Rodentia*

**FAMILY:** *Cricetidae*

**SUBFAMILY:** *Arvicolinae*

## BY THE NUMBERS

| | |
|---|---|
| **2** | *Average lifespan in years* |
| **6** | *Length in inches* |
| **13** | *Largest size of litter* |

### NUMEROUS IN NUMBERS

*A combination of multiple litters a year and plentiful food can lead to a population boom every three to four years. When this happens and groups become too large, they will migrate to find new food sources. This led to the myth that adult lemmings will jump off cliffs in large numbers to reduce the population density.*

### FAVORABLE FUR

*Sable pelts have been both valuable and popular since the Middle Ages. Its soft, rich, and silky textures have made it a luxury item for centuries. King Henry VIII of England declared that the sable pelt could only be worn by nobles. Today, they are still commonly hunted in Russia and commercially farmed.*

# 35. SABLE

Belonging to the marten species, sables are weasel-like carnivores. They are best known for their soft pelts that come in shades of brown and black. Pelts grow thicker and longer in the winter to adapt to the freezing temperatures. Sables have an endearing look with their rounded heads, large ears, and small black eyes and noses. If you have hopes to spot one, your chances are best at twilight when active hunting takes place. Their diet consists of rodents, fish, hares, and slugs. They have excellent climbing skills to aid their hunt. Home for sables is in dense forests of spruce, cedar, and birch, where they like to burrow in tree roots.

## BY THE NUMBERS

| | |
|---|---|
| **18** | *Lifespan in years they can reach in the wild* |
| **7.5** | *Distance they can travel in miles a day to search for food when scarce* |
| **22** | *The length in inches they can reach* |

### PREGNANCY

*Like humans, sables have a gestation period of about nine months. Unlike humans, it's normal for a sable to have up to seven cubs in a litter. Another amazing difference is that a female can postpone her pregnancy due to delayed embryonic development. Cub development only takes 25-30 days, but the mother can delay the development due to environmental conditions.*

# 36. HOARY REDPOLL

A black chin, orange bill, and gray feathers with light brown streaks are what to look for when searching for a hoary redpoll. This small finch breed inhabits the High Arctic and bushy areas of the tundra, using shrubs and small willows as nesting sites. When breeding season approaches, redpolls can occasionally be found at bird feeders in more southern regions of Canada. Nyjer, or black-oil sunflower seeds, are a redpoll delight. Redpolls can be curious about settlements and tame around people, sometimes even landing on them. Their main predators are larger birds of prey and carnivorous scavengers like foxes.

## CLASSIFICATION

**KINGDOM:** *Animalia*

**PHYLUM:** *Arthropoda*

**CLASS:** *Insecta*

**ORDER:** *Lepidoptera*

**SUPERFAMILY:** *Noctuoidea*

**FAMILY:** *Erebidae*

**GENUS:** *Gynaephora*

**SPECIES:** *G. groenlandica*

## BY THE NUMBERS

| | |
|---|---|
| **7** YEARS | *Average lifespan* |
| **5** | *Usual number of eggs in a clutch* |
| **7** OUNCES | *Average weight of an adult* |

## LAYERS OF COMFORT

*Due to the extreme weather, the hoary redpoll keeps warm with more feathered body coverage than most other birds. If a warm spell does happen to hit the Arctic tundra, the redpoll simply plucks out enough feathers to reach a comfortable body temperature, with new feathers able to grow back in a matter of days.*

# 37. ARCTIC SHREW

The tri-colored fur of Arctic shrews helps to differentiate them from mice and other small rodents. They have red-tipped teeth, a round body shape, and a noticeably long snout. If you are still unsure of the identity of an Arctic shrew, its pungent body odor is sure to give it away! Shrews tend to live solitary lives near bodies of water that range from the Arctic Circle to the northern United States. They are constantly on the hunt for food, trying to keep pace with their quick metabolism. Insects like larch sawflies are a major source of their carnivorous diet. The only true predator of the Arctic shrew is the owl.

## CLASSIFICATION

**KINGDOM:** *Animalia*

**PHYLUM:** *Chordata*

**CLASS:** *Mammalia*

**ORDER:** *Eulipotyphla*

**FAMILY:** *Soricidae*

**GENUS:** *Sorex*

**SPECIES:** *S. arcticus*

## BY THE NUMBERS

| | |
|---|---|
| **32** | *The number of teeth of an Arctic shrew* |
| **7** | *Number of offspring per litter* |
| **50** | *The percentage of young shrews that die in their first month of life* |

## THEY ARE SO CUTE!

*You might be tempted to ask your parents for a pet shrew. After all, they look like mice, and mice make great pets. While they might rank high in the cute category, a shrew would not make a good pet. Its short lifespan would be difficult to adjust to, and its aggressive nature would lead to venomous bites. The venom won't harm a human, but it will hurt!*

## NEVER LOST IN THE DARK

*Night is the prime time to hunt for the red fox. Their eyes have an extra layer called the* tapetum lucidum *that reflects light back through the eye, giving them adaptive night vision. If night vision wasn't cool enough, red fox eyes glow green when light is shone into them at night!*

# 38. RED FOX

The red fox is an amazing Arctic creature! Belonging to the dog family with wolves and coyotes, it's no wonder the red fox is athletic. They can swim, clear six-foot fences, and run up to 31 mph. Food can be scarce at times in the northern part of the globe, and competition can be fierce, so their natural spryness is essential for survival. Super-hearing is another helpful adaptation. They can hear a crow flying from ⅓ mile away and a mouse squeak from 100 meters away. When taking a rest from hunting, red foxes can relax in their underground burrows or above ground in cozy hollows.

## CLASSIFICATION

**KINGDOM:** *Animalia*

**PHYLUM:** *Chordata*

**CLASS:** *Mammalia*

**ORDER:** *Carnivora*

**FAMILY:** *Canidae*

**GENUS:** *Vulpes*

**SPECIES:** *V. vulpes*

## BY THE NUMBERS

| | |
|---|---|
| **2** | *Number of weeks before fox cubs can open their eyes* |
| **8** | *Size in square miles the fox's territory can extend* |
| **5** | *Number of toes on their forepaws; their hind feet have only four toes* |

### SISTER ASSISTANCE

*Female foxes are called "vixen." Occasionally, the vixen will have some extra help in rearing her cubs. A non-breeding sister, for instance, will help the mother in her responsibilities while gaining valuable experience to successfully rear her own litter the next season.*

# 39. ARCTIC MOSQUITO

**I**f you ever visit the Arctic tundra in the summer, be sure to cover up! Mosquitoes in the Arctic are a larger and more furry version of their non-Arctic cousins. While the males feed on water and nectar, the females will seek a blood meal. Any warm-blooded creature, from humans to caribou to polar bears, will satisfy a female mosquito. Their eggs lay dormant in the frozen water until longer days of sunshine warm the temperature, bringing the mosquitos to life. Lots of wetlands and melted ice and snow are full of rich, organic material, providing plentiful food for the ever-growing mosquito population.

## ANNOYING ADVERSARY

*A well-understood fact is that mosquitos of any kind are a nuisance to people and animals alike. They are especially bothersome to the caribou of the Arctic, causing potential harm to herds. Caribou will move away from insect activity to find relief. Often, their movement will be toward windy areas that have little food or low-quality food, affecting the caribous' health.*

## CLASSIFICATION

**KINGDOM:** *Animalia*

**PHYLUM:** *Arthropoda*

**CLASS:** *Insecta*

**ORDER:** *Diptera*

**SUPERFAMILY:** *Culicoidea*

**FAMILY:** *Culicidae*

## BY THE NUMBERS

| | |
|---|---|
| **50** | *estimated percent of mosquito population increase if the Arctic temperatures rise two degrees Celsius* |
| **60** | *average egg count of a female mosquito* |
| **2** | *average lifespan in weeks* |

# 40. SEA OTTER

Adorable, goofy, and intelligent—all describe the beloved otter! These cold-water mammals are fun to watch and are incredibly social. About 90% of the world's otter population lives off the coast of Alaska. Here, you rarely see an otter on its own. They can be found in rafts (groups) of up to 1,000. To keep from drifting while they sleep atop the water, otters will hold paws or wrap themselves and their pups in kelp, making a makeshift raft. Their teeth arc twice as strong as human teeth to help crush urchins and crabs, allowing them to eat the necessary 25% of their body weight a day.

## CLASSIFICATION

**KINGDOM:** *Animalia*

**PHYLUM:** *Chordata*

**CLASS:** *Mammalia*

**ORDER:** *Carnivora*

**FAMILY:** *Mustelidae*

**SUBFAMILY:** *Lutrinae*

**GENUS:** *Enhydra*

**SPECIES:** *E. lutris*

## BY THE NUMBERS

| | |
|---|---|
| **5** | *Length of time in minutes they can hold their breath underwater* |
| **100** | *Weight in pounds of a male otter* |
| **1** | *The number of pups born to a female a year* |

## FANTASTIC FUR

*Otters can live their entire lives without ever leaving the water! One reason they can do this is the amazing protection of their fur. Otter fur has an estimated one million hairs per square inch, making it the densest fur of any animal worldwide. Such fur keeps otters comfortable in frigid waters since they don't have blubber like other large marine animals.*

## ABOUT THE AUTHOR

Christin is the author of several books for kids, including many in the Little Library of Natural History. She lives with her family in California, where she enjoys rollerblading, puzzles, and a good book.

**BUSHEL
& PECK
BOOKS**

## ABOUT THE
## PUBLISHER

Bushel & Peck Books is a children's publishing house with a special mission. Through our Book-for-Book Promise™, we donate one book to kids in need for every book we sell. Our beautiful books are given to kids through schools, libraries, local neighborhoods, shelters, nonprofits, and also to many selfless organizations who are working hard to make a difference. So thank you for purchasing this book! Because of you, another book will find itself in the hands of a child who needs it most.

Printed in the United States
by Baker & Taylor Publisher Services